MY FIRST TRIP TO A BASEBALL GAME/

MI PRIMER PARTIDO DE BÉISBOL

By Katie Kawa   Traducción al español: Eduardo Alamán

Gareth Stevens
Publishing

Please visit our website, www.garethstevens.com. For a free color catalog of all our high-quality books, call toll free 1-800-542-2595 or fax 1-877-542-2596.

Library of Congress Cataloging-in-Publication Data

Kawa, Katie.
My first trip to a baseball game = Mi primer partido de béisbol / Katie Kawa. — Bilingual ed.
   p. cm. — (My first adventures / Mis primeras aventuras)
ISBN 978-1-4339-7374-1 (library binding)
1. Baseball—Juvenile literature. I. Title. II. Title: Mi primer partido de béisbol.
GV867.5.K385 2012
796.357—dc23

2011048797

First Edition

Published in 2013 by
Gareth Stevens Publishing
111 East 14th Street, Suite 349
New York, NY 10003

Editor: Katie Kawa
Designer: Andrea Davison-Bartolotta
Spanish Translation: Eduardo Alamán

All Illustrations by Planman Technologies

Printed in the United States of America

CPSIA compliance information: Batch #CS12GS: For further information contact Gareth Stevens, New York, New York at 1-800-542-2595.

Contents

- -

Contenido

Today I am going
to a baseball game.

Hoy, voy a un partido
de béisbol.

My family and I go
to the baseball park.
This is where
our team plays.

Voy con mi familia al
parque de pelota.
Ahí es donde juega
nuestro equipo.

7

My dad holds
our tickets.
They tell us
where to sit.

Mi papá tiene los
boletos. Los boletos nos
dicen dónde debemos
sentarnos.

We get food to eat.
My mom and dad
eat hot dogs.

Compramos comida.
Papá y mamá comen
hot dogs.

I get ice cream.

Yo como helado.

13

The game is lots of fun!

¡El partido es
muy divertido!

TEN

MOYER 24

15

First, one player throws the ball. He is called the pitcher.

Primero, un jugador lanza la pelota. Este es el lanzador.

17

Then, a player hits the ball. He is called the batter.

Luego, un jugador le pega a la pelota. Este es el bateador.

19

One player hits the ball
over the wall.
It is a home run!

Un jugador ha volado
la pelota sobre el muro.
¡Es un cuadrangular!

Our team won
the game!

¡Nuestro equipo ha
ganado el partido!

23

Words to Know/
Palabras que debes saber

batter/
(el) bateador

pitcher/
(el) lanzador

tickets/
(los) boletos

Index / Índice